ALAN LARSON

# You are overthinking, again

*Using The Four A's To Live In The Moment, Avoid Negative Deepstate, Reduce Stress and Free The Mind*

# Contents

# Introduction

Why should you care? You're about to discover how to handle those pesky thoughts and feelings that just won't go away.

Have you ever felt like your brain is stuck on repeat, thinking about the same things over and over? That's what people usually call "overthinking." But guess what? Overthinking isn't just thinking a lot—it's more like being trapped in a maze of thoughts that never seem to lead anywhere useful.

It's like getting caught in a sticky spiderweb of worries and "what-ifs." And sometimes, it can feel really hard to find a way out. But don't worry! Just like you can learn to ride a bike or tie your shoes, you can learn to manage these tricky thoughts, too.

This book is your guide to understanding what happens in your mind when you overthink. We'll explore simple, fun ways to help you break free from that thought loop and feel more calm, clear, and in control.

Whether you sometimes feel like your brain is buzzing with too many thoughts, or you're just curious about how to handle them better, this book will walk you through it, step by step. So, are you ready to find out what's really going on inside your head and learn how to make peace with your thoughts? Let's dive in and get started on your journey to a clearer, happier mind!

# 1

## Chapter 1

## Getting Better at Handling Our Thoughts

Imagine your mind is like a big, twisty maze. When you overthink, it's like wandering around in that maze, bumping into dead ends and getting lost, no matter how hard you try to find the right path. Overthinking can make you feel tired, worried, and keep you up at night. It can even mess with your relationships and make life feel harder than it needs to be.

Some of us are more likely to overthink because of who we are, and sometimes it's because of what's happening around us. But here's the thing: often, we react to what we think is stressful, not what really is. Our brains can trick us into believing things are worse than they actually are. When we get stuck in these thought loops, it can feel overwhelming. But guess what? Just like learning how to ride a bike, we can learn how to handle our thoughts better.

It might be tricky at first to realize when you're overthinking. It's like trying to spot a tiny ant in a big garden. But noticing it is the first step to feeling better. To get there, we need to pay attention to how our thoughts, feelings, and the people around us all mix together. This means being curious about why we feel the way we do and asking ourselves questions to understand our emotions better. As we practice this, we start to trust ourselves more, and little by little, we can break the habit of overthinking.

Everyone feels stressed sometimes, but worrying doesn't have to take over our lives. Before you get caught up in a whirlwind of anxious thoughts, you can pause, take a deep breath, and gently challenge those thoughts. By doing this, you create a calm space in your mind where you can think clearly and feel more peaceful.

As you practice these new ways of thinking, you might notice that your mind starts to feel like a more peaceful place. Instead of getting stuck in that confusing maze of thoughts, you'll find yourself walking on a clearer path. It's not about stopping your thoughts completely—that's impossible! It's about guiding them in a way that helps you feel more in control and less overwhelmed. You'll begin to notice when you're starting to overthink and have the tools to gently steer your mind back to a calmer, more focused state.

Remember, this is a journey, and it's okay to take small steps. Sometimes you might slip back into old habits, and that's perfectly normal. The important thing is to keep practicing and be kind to yourself along the way. As you learn to manage your thoughts better, you'll also start to see how this affects other areas of your life. You may feel more confident in making decisions, more connected in your relationships, and more at peace with yourself. So, let's continue exploring these strategies together and discover how you can build a happier, healthier mind!

2

# Chapter 2

## The Four A's: Your New Superpowers for a Better Life

Sometimes, overthinking can make you feel like shouting, "AAAA!" But guess what? That "AAAA" can actually help you remember four super important strategies: **Avoid**, **Alter**, **Accept**, and **Adapt**. These are your new tools to handle life's challenges and keep your mind calm and clear.

Let's start with **Avoiding**. Imagine life throws a curve ball your way—it could be a tough situation, a noisy place, or even someone who makes you feel anxious. It's okay to step back or walk away when things get too stressful. If you know something or someone is going to make you feel bad, try to avoid it. For example, if there's a friend who always makes you nervous, it's perfectly fine to spend less time with them. Or if loud sounds bother you, find quieter spots where you can feel more at peace. Remember, avoiding isn't about running away; it's about protecting your own well-being and knowing when to say "no" to things that don't serve you.

Next, let's talk about Altering . Sometimes, you can't just walk away from a problem, but you can change how it affects you. If someone or something is making you upset, try talking about it. Use your voice to make things better. Whether it's asking for help, setting boundaries, or finding a new way to look at the situation, you often have more power to change things than you might think. Speaking up and making small changes can lead to big improvements in how you feel and how you handle stress.

But, of course, not everything can be changed. That's where **Accepting** comes in. Some things are just out of your control, and that's okay! Accepting doesn't mean you like what's happening—it means you understand that you can't control everything. When you accept the things you can't change, you free yourself from a lot of frustration. You start to focus on what you can control— like your thoughts and reactions—and that can make a huge difference in how you feel.

Finally, we have **Adapting**. Life is always changing, and sometimes we need to change with it. Adapting means being flexible and finding ways to stay positive, even when things are tough. It's about looking for the bright side and finding hope, even in difficult situations. Adapting isn't always easy, but it makes you stronger and helps you handle whatever life throws your way.

As you continue to practice the Four A's, you'll notice that these strategies can be like having a toolkit for your mind. When something stressful happens, instead of feeling overwhelmed, you can reach into your mental toolkit and decide which "A" will help you the most in that moment. Maybe you need to Avoid a situation that's too overwhelming, or perhaps it's time to **Alter** how you're dealing with a problem. Sometimes, just Accepting what's out of your hands is enough to bring peace, and Adapting can help you find a way forward, even in challenging times.

The beauty of these tools is that they can be mixed and matched depending on what life throws at you. You might need to use more than one "A" at a time, and that's perfectly okay. For example, you might **Accept** that a situation can't be changed, but then **Adapt** your mindset to focus on something positive.

Or you might **Avoid** a stressor while also **Altering** your environment to make it more peaceful. The more you practice using the Four A's, the more natural it will become, and soon enough, you'll find that managing stress and overthinking isn't as hard as it once seemed. You'll have more confidence, more clarity, and a greater sense of control over your life.

By using the Four A's—Avoid, Alter, Accept, and Adapt—you'll be better equipped to handle stress and keep your mind clear. These strategies aren't about ignoring problems; they're about facing them in a way that protects your peace and helps you grow. As you practice these new skills, you'll start to see how they can transform not just your thoughts, but your whole outlook on life. Ready to put your new superpowers to work? Let's keep going!

# 3

# Chapter 3

## Mindfulness: Your Magic Wand for Overthinking

Imagine you had a magic wand that could help you calm your mind whenever it gets too noisy. Well, you do—it's called mindfulness! Mindfulness is all about paying attention to what's happening right now, without getting lost in worries about the past or the future. It's like pressing the pause button on your thoughts and just being present in the moment.

When you practice mindfulness, you're training your brain to focus on what's real and right in front of you, instead of getting tangled up in a web of "what-ifs" and "maybes." For example, when you're eating your favourite snack, try to really notice the taste, the smell, and the texture. Or when you're outside, pay attention to the colours of the leaves or the sound of the birds. These little moments of focus help you stay grounded and stop overthinking from taking over.

One of the great things about mindfulness is that it's something you can do anytime, anywhere. Whether you're brushing your teeth, walking to school, or just sitting quietly, you can practice being mindful. The more you do it, the easier it gets, and the more you'll find that your mind doesn't race as much. It's like giving your brain a gentle break from all the noise and stress.

Another powerful part of mindfulness is learning to notice your thoughts without judging them. Sometimes, we get caught up in thinking that our worries or fears are "bad" or that we shouldn't be having them. But with mindfulness, you can learn to observe your thoughts like clouds floating by in the sky. They're there, but they don't have to control you. You can watch them come and go without getting stuck on any one thought.

As you build your mindfulness skills, you might notice that you start to feel more peaceful and less reactive. Instead of getting upset when something doesn't go your way, you'll be able to take a deep breath, focus on the present, and respond with a clear mind. Mindfulness helps you create a little space between your thoughts and your reactions, giving you the power to choose how you want to respond.

Over time, mindfulness can transform how you experience the world. It's like discovering a secret superpower that helps you stay calm, focused, and in control, no matter what's happening around you. By practicing mindfulness regularly, you'll find that overthinking has less of a grip on your mind, and you'll be able to enjoy life more fully, one moment at a time.

Incorporating mindfulness into your daily routine doesn't have to be complicated. Start with just a few minutes each day, and gradually build up as you become more comfortable with it. Whether through deep breathing, mindful walking, or simply paying attention to your surroundings, every little bit helps. Before you know it, you'll have a new tool to keep overthinking at bay and bring more calm into your life.

Mindfulness is a journey, not a destination. Be patient with yourself as you learn and grow. Each moment of mindfulness is a step toward a clearer, more peaceful mind. So, take a deep breath, let go of any stress, and enjoy the present moment—because that's where the magic really happens!

As you deepen your mindfulness practice, you might begin to notice subtle changes in how you interact with the world around you. Situations that once triggered anxiety or stress may start to feel more manageable. This is because mindfulness helps you build resilience—a kind of mental strength that allows you to handle challenges with greater ease. Instead of feeling overwhelmed by your thoughts or emotions, you'll find that you can observe them calmly, decide what's worth your attention, and let go of what isn't.

Mindfulness also brings a sense of appreciation to everyday life. When you're fully present, even the simplest activities can become sources of joy and contentment. Whether it's savouring the taste of your morning coffee, feeling the warmth of the sun on your skin, or listening to your favourite song, mindfulness helps you truly experience these moments. This shift in perspective can make your days feel richer and more fulfilling, as you start to notice and enjoy the little things that often go unnoticed.

Another important aspect of mindfulness is its ability to foster compassion—both for yourself and others. By practicing non-judgmental awareness, you learn to treat yourself with kindness, especially when you're struggling with overthinking or difficult emotions. Instead of criticizing yourself for having these thoughts, you can acknowledge them with understanding and self-compassion. This same approach can extend to others, helping you become more patient, empathetic, and supportive in your relationships. As you cultivate this compassionate mindset, you'll not only ease your mental burden but also create a more positive and peaceful environment for those around you.

4

# Chapter 4

## Breaking Free from Negative Thoughts

Have you ever felt like you're stuck in a storm of negative thoughts, where everything feels gloomy and nothing seems to go right? It's like having a dark cloud follow you around, making it hard to see the sunshine. But don't worry—there are ways to break free from these negative thoughts and find your way back to a brighter, happier place.

First, let's understand that negative thoughts are a part of life. Everyone has them from time to time, and that's okay. The important thing is not to let them take over your mind. When you start feeling like your thoughts are dragging you down, try to pause and notice what's happening. Ask yourself, "Is this thought really true?" or "Is there another way to look at this?" Often, you'll find that your mind is just playing tricks on you, making things seem worse than they really are.

One helpful trick is to talk back to those negative thoughts. Imagine that they're just like a bully trying to make you feel bad. You wouldn't let a bully push you around, so don't let your negative thoughts do it either! Instead, stand up to them by thinking of something positive or reminding yourself of the good things in your life. You can even say to yourself, "I'm stronger than these thoughts, and I choose to focus on the positive."

Another way to fight off negative thoughts is to distract yourself with something fun or interesting. When your mind is busy with something you enjoy, like playing a game, reading a book, or spending time with friends, there's no room for those negative thoughts to sneak in. Doing things you love can lift your spirits and help you see the bright side of life again.

And remember, you don't have to do it all alone. If you're feeling overwhelmed by negative thoughts, it's okay to talk to someone you trust, like a parent, teacher, or friend. They can offer support and help you see things from a different perspective. Sometimes, just sharing what's on your mind can make a big difference in how you feel.

Breaking free from negative thoughts takes practice, but the more you do it, the easier it gets. Over time, you'll become better at noticing when negative thoughts creep in and knowing how to push them away. You'll start to see that the stormy clouds in your mind can pass, and the sun will shine again. So keep practicing, stay positive, and remember that you have the power to control your thoughts and create a happier, more peaceful mind.

As you keep practicing how to handle negative thoughts, you'll discover that they lose their power over you. Instead of feeling like they're in charge, you'll start to realize that *you* are the one in control. This doesn't mean that negative thoughts will disappear completely—they're still going to pop up from time to time. But now, you'll have the tools to manage them better. It's like being the captain of a ship: even when the waves get rough, you know how to steer your ship safely through the storm.

Another important thing to remember is that it's okay to have bad days. We all do! Sometimes, no matter how hard we try, it's tough to shake off those negative feelings. On days like these, be kind to yourself. Instead of getting upset or frustrated, remind yourself that it's normal to feel this way sometimes. Give yourself permission to take it easy and do something that makes you feel good, like watching your favorite movie, drawing, or just taking a nap. Taking care of yourself during these times is important, and it can help you bounce back even stronger.

Finally, one of the best ways to keep negative thoughts at bay is to focus on gratitude. When you make it a habit to think about the things you're thankful for, it becomes harder for negativity to take over. Try writing down a few things each day that make you happy—like a tasty meal, a kind word from a friend, or even just a sunny day. Gratitude is like a superpower that can brighten your mood and help you see the good in every situation. The more you practice it, the more you'll notice all the wonderful things around you, and the easier it will be to keep those negative thoughts away.

# 5

# Chapter 5

## Using a SMART Checklist to Reach Your Goals

Do you ever feel like your days are so packed with things to do that you don't know where to start? It can be like juggling a bunch of balls at once, and sometimes, it seems like there's just not enough time in the day. But guess what? You can handle everything on your plate with a little help from something called a SMART checklist!

Imagine you have a big list of things you want to do or achieve. A SMART checklist can help you turn that list into a clear plan. SMART stands for Specific, Measurable, Attainable, Relevant, and Time-bound. Let's break these words down to see how they can help you:

- Specific means being clear about what you want. Instead of saying, "I want to get better at math," you could say, "I want to finish my math homework every day." This makes your goal easier to understand and follow.

- Measurable means you should be able to track your progress. For example, if your goal is to read more books, you could keep track of how many books you read each month. This way, you can see how well you're doing.

- Attainable means your goal should be something you can actually reach. If you want to improve in soccer, setting a goal to practice kicking the ball for 15 minutes each day is more realistic than saying you'll become a professional player in a week.

- Relevant means your goal should be important to you. If you love drawing, setting a goal to draw a new picture every week is relevant to your interests and will keep you motivated.

- Time-bound means you should set a deadline for your goal. Instead of saying, "I want to get better at science," you could say, "I want to complete my science project by next Friday." Having a deadline helps you stay focused and organized.

With your SMART goals in mind, it's easier to see what you need to do each day. Make a plan, write down your goals, and use a calendar or a to-do list to keep track. This will help you stay on top of your tasks and make sure you're using your time wisely.

Feeling tired or overwhelmed? It's important to take breaks and rest. Don't forget to make time for fun activities and say no to things that make you feel stressed. If you have too much to do, ask for help from friends or family members you trust. They can share the load and make things easier.

Remember, the goal is to spend your time on what you care about most. By setting SMART goals and organizing your schedule, you can make every day count and enjoy more of the things you love. So, grab your planner and start making your SMART goals today—you've got this!

Now that you have a plan, let's explore some easy ways to clear your mind and stay focused.

# 6

# Chapter 6

## Calm Your Mind and Body with Visualization and Muscle Relaxation

When you're feeling stressed and need to calm down quickly, sometimes just talking about it isn't enough. Luckily, there are fun and easy ways to help you relax using both your imagination and your body. Two great methods to try are visualization and progressive muscle relaxation (PMR). By combining these techniques, you can help your mind and body feel more relaxed and peaceful.

First, let's start with visualization. This is like taking a mini-vacation in your mind. Close your eyes and take slow, deep breaths. Imagine a place that makes you feel happy and relaxed, like a sunny beach or a cosy treehouse. Picture yourself there, enjoying the sights, sounds, and smells. You might hear the gentle waves of the ocean, feel the soft sand under your feet, or smell the salty sea air. The more you imagine, the more relaxed you'll feel.

After you've enjoyed your mental getaway for five to ten minutes, imagine folding up this happy place and putting it in your pocket. You can bring it out anytime you need a break! When you're ready to finish, slowly open your eyes and stretch your body. Take a few deep breaths and notice how calm and refreshed you feel. With a bit of practice, you'll be able to use this technique whenever you need to unwind.

Now, let's talk about progressive muscle relaxation. This method helps you become aware of how your muscles feel and teaches you to relax them. Sit or lie down comfortably and close your eyes. Start with your toes and work your way up through your body. Tense each muscle group for about ten seconds, then relax it. For example, clench your fists tight and count to ten, then let go and feel the tension melt away. Move on to your arms, shoulders, and so on, until you've relaxed your whole body. After finishing, take a few deep breaths and stretch out. You'll find that your muscles are looser and your mind feels clearer.

## Create a Relaxing Routine with Deep Breathing and Stretching

Adding a relaxing routine to your daily life can make a big difference in how you feel. Simple activities like deep breathing and stretching can help you stay calm and happy. Here's how you can create your own relaxing routine:

Start with deep breathing. Sit in a comfy spot and close your eyes. Breathe in slowly through your nose, counting to four. Hold your breath for a count of four, and then breathe out slowly through your mouth, also counting to four. This is called the "4-4-4" breathing method. Doing this a few times can help your body relax and clear your mind.

Next, add some stretching to your routine. Stretching helps your muscles feel more relaxed and can make you feel more comfortable. Try stretching your arms high above your head, touching your toes, or doing a gentle twist to one side. Hold each stretch for a few seconds and breathe deeply. Stretching not only helps with relaxation but also keeps your body flexible and healthy.

By making deep breathing and stretching a regular part of your day, you'll start to notice that you feel more relaxed and less stressed. These simple activities are easy to do and can be done almost anywhere, making them perfect for a calming daily routine.

## The Power of Positive Self-Talk and Setting Goals

Another way to keep stress at bay is by practicing positive self-talk and setting goals. These two techniques can help you feel more confident and focused.

Positive self-talk is all about being kind to yourself with your words. When you make a mistake or face a challenge, instead of saying things like, "I'm terrible at this," try saying something positive like, "I'm learning and getting better." Positive self-talk helps you stay motivated and can make tough situations seem easier to handle.

Setting goals is also a great way to stay focused and reduce stress. Goals give you something to work towards and can help you organize your tasks. Start by setting small, achievable goals, like finishing a homework assignment or practicing a new skill. Celebrate your progress along the way and remember that every little step counts!

Together, positive self-talk and goal-setting can help you feel more in control and less overwhelmed. They are powerful tools that can turn stress into motivation and make challenges feel more manageable. So, keep talking positively to yourself and setting goals—you're on your way to success!

## Find Your Balance with Fun and Relaxation

Balancing fun and relaxation with your daily responsibilities is key to staying happy and healthy. Sometimes, it's easy to get caught up in tasks and forget to take time for yourself. But finding time for fun is just as important as getting things done!

Think about activities that make you happy and relaxed. It could be playing your favourite game, drawing, reading a book, or spending time with friends. Make sure to include these activities in your schedule, just like you would with schoolwork or chores. Having fun is a great way to take a break from stress and recharge your energy.

Creating a balance between work and play helps keep your mind and body in top shape. By scheduling time for both responsibilities and relaxation, you'll be able to handle your tasks better and enjoy life more. Remember, relaxation is not just about taking a break; it's an essential part of staying healthy and happy. So, don't forget to mix in some fun with your daily routine—your future self will thank you!

**Use Journaling and Creative Outlets to Manage Stress**

Another fun and effective way to manage stress is through journaling and creative outlets. Writing in a journal or engaging in creative activities can help you express your feelings and take a break from your worries.

Journaling is like having a conversation with yourself. You can write about your day, your thoughts, or anything that's on your mind. This helps you sort through your feelings and see things more clearly. Try writing in your journal regularly, and you might be surprised at how much better you feel after putting your thoughts on paper.

Creative outlets are activities that let you express yourself in a fun way. This could be drawing, painting, playing music, or crafting. Creative activities help you focus on something enjoyable and can be a great way to relax. They also allow you to explore your feelings and ideas in a different way.

By using journaling and creative outlets, you can find new ways to handle stress and feel more in control. These activities not only provide relaxation but also help you understand and manage your emotions better. So grab a journal or your favourite art supplies and start exploring—you might find that these creative practices are just what you need to feel more balanced and happy.

7

# Chapter 7

## How Cognitive Behavioral Therapy (CBT) Can Help You Clear Your Mental Clutter

Imagine your mind is like a messy attic. Over time, it can fill up with all sorts of unwanted stuff—old, dusty thoughts, and worries that just sit there taking up space. But guess what? You don't have to live with this mental clutter. If you're feeling stuck in a negative mindset or overwhelmed by self-doubt, it's time to try something called Cognitive Behavioral Therapy (CBT). CBT is like a cleaning crew for your brain that helps you sort through and tidy up those messy thoughts.

CBT works by shining a light on your "cognitive distortions" —these are tricky patterns of thinking that can make you feel worse. For example, you might catch yourself thinking things like, "I always mess things up," or "Nothing ever goes right." These thoughts are often exaggerated or overly negative. CBT helps you identify these patterns and shows you how to challenge them. It's like having a mental toolkit to fix broken beliefs and replace them with more realistic and positive ones.

To get started with CBT, you can keep a dysfunctional thought record. This is a simple way to track your negative thoughts and feelings. When you notice a negative emotion taking over, ask yourself some questions: "Did I look at the whole picture before making this judgment? Am I assuming something without evidence? Is this reaction based on a habit rather than a thoughtful choice?" By asking these questions, you can start to break down the negative thoughts and see if there are better ways to think about the situation. Write down at least three alternative thoughts or solutions that are more balanced and fair.

CBT isn't just about spotting negative thoughts; it's also about understanding why you feel the way you do and finding ways to make things better. By exploring how your emotions and thoughts interact, you can create healthier mental habits. For example, instead of jumping to the worst possible outcome, you can learn to approach situations with a more open and positive mindset. This approach helps you take control of your thoughts and feelings, making it easier to handle challenges and reduce stress.

So, are you ready to give your mind a makeover? Think of CBT as a fun adventure where you get to be the hero who clears out the mental clutter and makes room for positive and empowering thoughts. With practice and patience, you'll find that your brain feels lighter, more focused, and much more manageable. And who knows? You might even enjoy the process of discovering just how powerful your thoughts can be when you learn to guide them in the right direction.

**Turn Negative Thoughts into Positive Actions**

Once you start using Cognitive Behavioral Therapy (CBT), you'll find it's not just about changing how you think, but also about turning those new, positive thoughts into actions. It's like taking the clean, fresh space in your mental attic and filling it with things that make you happy and successful.

One way to do this is by setting small, achievable goals based on your new positive thoughts. For example, if you've been working on changing the belief "I'm not good enough" into "I'm capable and improving every day," set a goal that reflects this new belief. It could be something like trying out a new hobby, asking for help when you need it, or completing a challenging project. By taking action, you reinforce your new positive mindset and see real results.

Another important aspect of CBT is practicing self-compassion. This means being kind to yourself, especially when things don't go as planned. If you slip back into old thinking patterns or face setbacks, remind yourself that everyone makes mistakes and that learning and growing is a process. Treat yourself with the same kindness you would offer to a friend.

Additionally, celebrate your successes along the way. When you reach a goal or notice improvements in how you handle your thoughts, take a moment to acknowledge your achievements. Celebrating your progress helps keep you motivated and reinforces the positive changes you're making.

Practice Mindfulness and Self-Awareness

Combining CBT with mindfulness can make a big difference in managing your thoughts and emotions. Mindfulness is about being present in the moment and observing your thoughts without judgment. It's like taking a step back and watching your thoughts go by, rather than getting caught up in them.

Start by setting aside a few minutes each day for mindfulness practice. Find a quiet place to sit, close your eyes, and focus on your breathing. Notice how your breath feels as it moves in and out. When your mind starts to wander, gently bring your attention back to your breath. This simple practice can help you become more aware of your thoughts and feelings and respond to them in a more balanced way.

Incorporating mindfulness into daily activities can also help. Whether you're eating, walking, or even doing chores, try to stay fully engaged in the activity. Notice the details of what you're doing and how you're feeling. This practice helps you stay grounded and reduces the likelihood of getting caught up in negative thought patterns.

By combining CBT with mindfulness, you create a powerful toolkit for managing stress and improving your mental well-being. You'll find that you're better able to handle life's challenges with a clear, focused mind and a positive attitude.

Build a Support Network and Seek Professional Help

Even with CBT and mindfulness, sometimes it's helpful to have extra support. Building a support network of friends, family, and mentors can provide encouragement and perspective when you need it most. Share your goals and challenges with people you trust, and let them know how they can help you. Having a support system can make a big difference in staying motivated and feeling connected.

If you find that you need more help, seeking professional support from a therapist or counsellor can be a valuable step. Professionals can offer additional strategies and tools to help you manage your thoughts and emotions effectively. They can work with you to tailor techniques to your unique needs and provide guidance as you continue to grow.

Remember, seeking help is a sign of strength, not weakness. Everyone needs support at times, and reaching out can help you navigate challenges more effectively and lead a more fulfilling life.

By building a strong support network and seeking professional help when needed, you create a solid foundation for managing stress and achieving your goals. With the right tools and support, you'll be well on your way to a happier and more balanced life.

8

# Chapter 8

## The 5-4-3-2-1 Grounding Technique: A Simple Way to Calm Your Mind

Have you ever felt that overwhelming tightness in your chest or that racing feeling in your mind? This is called anxiety, and it's something many people experience at some point. It can be really uncomfortable and often seems to pop up out of nowhere. But don't worry, you're not alone, and there are ways to handle it.

One helpful method to quickly reduce anxiety is the 5-4-3-2-1 grounding technique. This technique is like a fun game that helps you shift your focus from anxious thoughts to the present moment. It works by engaging your senses, which can help you feel more grounded and calm. Here's how to play:

1. Start with Five Things You Can See: Look around and find five things to notice. These could be a colourful book, a potted plant, a cosy blanket, a picture on the wall, or a cup on the table. Just name them in your mind and pay attention to each one.

2. Next, Identify Four Things You Can Feel: Focus on what you can physically sense. Maybe you feel the texture of the chair you're sitting on, the warmth of a sweater, the cool breeze on your face, or the feeling of your feet touching the floor. Notice how these sensations make you feel more present.

3. Now, Listen for Three Sounds: What sounds can you hear around you? It might be the chirping of birds, the hum of a refrigerator, or the rustle of leaves outside. Paying attention to these sounds helps bring your attention back to the here and now.

4. Then, Notice Two Smells: Smell is a powerful sense. Try to identify two smells. It could be the aroma of your morning coffee, the scent of fresh flowers, or even the clean smell of the air after rain. Take a moment to really enjoy these smells.

5. Finally, Focus on One Taste: Think about something you're eating or drinking or even the taste left in your mouth. It could be the sweetness of a piece of fruit, the refreshing flavour of a sip of water, or the taste of minty toothpaste. Let this taste bring you back to the present.

By using the 5-4-3-2-1 technique, you're helping yourself break free from a cycle of anxious thoughts and grounding yourself in the present moment. It's like pressing a mental reset button, making it easier to calm down and refocus.

**Embrace Mindfulness and Self-Care**

In addition to grounding techniques, incorporating mindfulness and self-care into your daily routine can help manage anxiety and stress. Mindfulness means paying attention to your thoughts and feelings without judgment. It's about being present and fully engaged in what's happening right now.

Start with simple mindfulness practices, such as taking a few moments each day to focus on your breathing. Sit quietly, close your eyes, and take slow, deep breaths. Notice how your breath feels as it moves in and out. If your mind starts to wander, gently bring your focus back to your breath. This practice helps you stay calm and aware.

Self-care is also crucial for managing stress. This includes taking time for activities that you enjoy and that help you relax. Whether it's reading a book, going for a walk, or spending time with loved ones, make sure to include these activities in your schedule. Self-care isn't just about taking breaks; it's about prioritizing your well-being and finding joy in everyday moments.

By combining mindfulness and self-care with techniques like the 5-4-3-2-1 grounding method, you create a powerful toolkit for reducing anxiety and enhancing your overall mental health. These practices help you stay connected to the present moment and foster a positive mindset.

**Create a Personalized Stress-Relief Plan**

Developing a personalized stress-relief plan can help you manage anxiety and stress more effectively. Start by identifying what triggers your stress and what activities or techniques help you feel better. This might include grounding exercises, mindfulness practices, or self-care routines.

Make a list of your favourite stress-relief strategies and include them in your daily or weekly routine. For example, you might decide to use the 5-4-3-2-1 technique when you feel overwhelmed, practice mindfulness for a few minutes each day, and schedule regular self-care activities like taking a bath or enjoying a hobby.

Having a plan in place helps you respond to stress more effectively and ensures that you have reliable tools to turn to when you need them. Remember, everyone's stress-relief plan will look different, so find what works best for you and make it a regular part of your life.

# 9

# Conclusion

In this book, we've explored various techniques to help you manage stress and overcome the habit of overthinking. From understanding Cognitive Behavioral Therapy (CBT) to practicing mindfulness and using the 5-4-3-2-1 grounding technique, you now have a range of tools to support your mental well-being.

CBT helps you recognize and challenge negative thought patterns, allowing you to replace them with more balanced and positive beliefs. Mindfulness teaches you to stay present and aware, while the 5-4-3-2-1 technique offers a quick and engaging way to ground yourself during moments of anxiety.

By integrating these methods into your daily routine and creating a personalized stress-relief plan, you can build resilience and manage stress more effectively. Remember, the journey to a calmer and more balanced mind is ongoing. With practice and patience, you'll find yourself better equipped to handle life's challenges and enjoy greater peace of mind. Embrace these techniques, make them your own, and let them guide you towards a more relaxed and fulfilling life.